Handwriting

Practice Paper

This book belongs to :

....

....

CPSIA information can be obtained
at www.ICGtesting.com
Printed in the USA
LVHW061124091220
673659LV00033B/729

9 781716 382017